Illustrated
Stories *from the* Bible

Volume 10

AUTHORS
George and Marilyn Durrant
Former Professor of Ancient Scriptures

Doctor of Education

ARTIST AND ART DIRECTOR
Vernon Murdock
Artist Illustrator

Bachelor of Fine Arts
Graduate Work, University of Madrid,
    Spain

CORRELATORS AND DIRECTORS
Steven R. Shallenberger, *President*
Community Press, Wisdom House, Eagle
    Marketing Corporation

Bachelor of Science; Accounting, Business
SCMP, Graduate School of Business, Harvard
    University

Paul R. Cheesman
Director of Scripture in Religious Study Center
Chaplain, U.S. Navy

Doctor of Religious Education

Lael J. Woodbury
Chairman, National Committee on Royalties,
    American Theatre Association

Doctor of Philosophy, University of Illinois

ADVISORS
Dale T. Tingey
Director of American Indian Services and
    Research Center

Doctor of Philosophy, Guidance and
    Counseling; Washington State University

Reverend Raymond E. Ansel
Ordained Minister

Southwestern Assemblies of God College, Texas
Berean Bible School, Missouri

Millie Foster Cheesman
Writer, Poetess

Reverend William R. Schroeder
United Church of Christ

United Theological Seminary of the Twin Cities
    New Brighton, Minnesota

FIRST EDITION VOLUME 10, 1982
Second Printing February 1984

Lithographed in U.S.A.
by
COMMUNITY PRESS, INC.
P.O. Box 1229
Antioch, California 94509

A Member of
The American Bookseller's Association
New York, New York

Behold, I stand at the door, and knock: if any man hear my voice, and open the door, I will come in to him, and will sup with him, and he with me.

To him that overcometh will I grant to sit with me in my throne, even as I also overcame, and am set down with my Father in his throne.

Revelation 3:20, 21

Dedicated to boys and girls throughout the world and to all who love the Bible.

A nondenominational work.

CONTENTS

Our story so far.. 7

Given From the Heart (The Widow's Mite) 8

Helping Versus Hurting (The Least of These and the Betrayal)......... 12

The Last Supper (Washing Feet and Peter's Promise) 18

The Last Supper Continues (Love One Another) 22

Jesus Takes Our Sins Upon Him (The Garden of Gethsemane and the Arrest) 27

That We Can Live Again (The Arrest)................................. 32

Close to the End (The Trial) 39

The Sorrow of an Unkept Promise (Peter's Denial) 40

King of the Jews (Jesus Before Pilate).............................. 46

Silent Suffering (Jesus Before Herod) 50

The Saddest Sentence (Pilate Gives In).............................. 52

That Which Cannot Be Washed Away (The Scourging of Jesus) 57

The Saddest of All Times (The Crucifixion) 60

The Happiest of All Times (The Resurrection) 67

The First To Know (Mary Sees the Resurrected Christ) 72

Our Hearts Can Burn Within Us (The Disciples on the Road to Emmaus)...... 79

To Be a Special Witness (Jesus Appears to the Apostles)............. 82

We Know Him With Our Hearts (Thomas Doubts) 84

The Power To Begin (Jesus Promises the Holy Ghost and Is Taken into Heaven)..... 87

A Link With Heaven (The Holy Ghost) 92

The Outpouring of the Holy Spirit (The Day of Pentecost) 94

In the Name of Jesus Christ (Peter Heals a Lame Man)............... 100

Giving One's Life (Stephen Dies for the Cause of Truth) 104

The Gospel of Jesus Is for All People (The Story of Cornelius) 110

A Mighty Leader (Peter) 117

From Persecuting to Preaching (Saul's Conversion) 124

The Future (The Book of Revelation)................................ 135

Looking Ahead 136

Our story so far . . .

As we think back, we recall that when Adam and Eve walked away from the Garden of Eden, they longed for the day when they could return to their former happiness. Through the promptings of the Holy Spirit, they knew that someday God would free them from the sorrow and bondage of their sins.

We remember that Noah was brokenhearted with the wickedness of the people in his day. He also looked forward to the time when the hearts of men would change toward goodness.

Each of the prophets—Abraham, Isaac, Jacob, Joseph, Moses, Isaiah, Ezekiel, and others—knew that someday a Messiah would come to save the people from the grip of Satan and to help them find the joy that comes in keeping the commandments of the Lord.

We learned that Jesus was born in a stable in Bethlehem. After growing to maturity in Galilee, he was baptized by John the Baptist. He chose and trained twelve humble followers to be leaders. He taught in parables, performed miracles, and was loved by his followers.

As we read on the next pages, the time has come for Jesus to suffer, bleed, and die. But his sacrifice frees us all from mortal death and from sin, if we repent.

We will be saddened by his death, but we will rejoice in his resurrection and his promise to someday return. We will see how Peter, Paul, and the other apostles continued to teach his gospel of truth and freedom after his death.

As we turn the final page, we will know that the story has not ended, but that it is continually unfolding each day of our lives.

GIVEN FROM THE HEART
The Widow's Mite

Two days had passed since Jesus had entered the city of Jerusalem. On this day, like many days before, the scribes and Pharisees, bitter with jealousy toward Jesus, continued looking for a reason to arrest him.

As a small group gathered around Jesus in the temple, one Jewish leader tried to prove that Jesus was disloyal to their Roman leader, Caesar. He eagerly spoke to Jesus, "We know you do not feel that one man is better than another. You treat all men the same. Also, you have said before that tribute should not be paid to any man but only to God."

> Tell us therefore, What thinkest thou? Is it lawful [for us] to give tribute [tax money] unto Cæsar . . . [or do you feel that he is no better than us and that we should not have to give him tribute money]?
>
> Matthew 22:17

But Jesus was far wiser than the scribes and Pharisees. He quietly considered his answer before speaking.

> Shew me the tribute money. And they brought unto him a penny.
> And he saith unto them, Whose *is* this image [picture] and superscription [writing]?

> They say unto him, Cæsar's. Then saith he unto them, Render [give] therefore unto Cæsar the things which are Cæsar's; and unto God the things that are God's.
>
> Matthew 22:19-21

The man who had been so certain that he could trick Jesus knew that his plan had not succeeded. Everyone present marveled at Jesus' wisdom.

Sitting near the treasury, Jesus saw "how the people cast money into the treasury: and many that were rich cast in much." (Mark 12:41) As Jesus watched, a poor widow threw in two mites. A mite had less value than any other coin in their land.

> And he called *unto him* his disciples, and saith unto them . . . That this poor widow hath cast more in [given more], than all they which have cast [much more money] into the treasury.

> Mark 12:43

The rich had given only a small part of what they had; but the widow had given money she needed to use for food.

The disciples learned an important lesson that day. Perhaps we might ask ourselves, "Am I like the widow, willing to give all that I have because of my love for God and because of my faith in him?"

HELPING VERSUS HURTING
The Least of These and the Betrayal

Jesus told the people that at some future time he would return to the earth. He told them to be ready for him by keeping his commandments, living good lives, using their talents wisely, and helping others.

He told his listeners that someday each of them would stand before God to be judged. He said,

. . . and he shall separate them [the people] one from another, as a shepherd divideth *his* sheep from the goats:

And he shall set the sheep [those who followed his teachings] on his right hand, but the goats [those who did not follow his teachings] on the left.

Then shall the King say unto them on his right hand, Come, ye blessed of my Father, inherit the kingdom [of heaven which has been] prepared for you from the foundation of the world.

Matthew 25:32-34

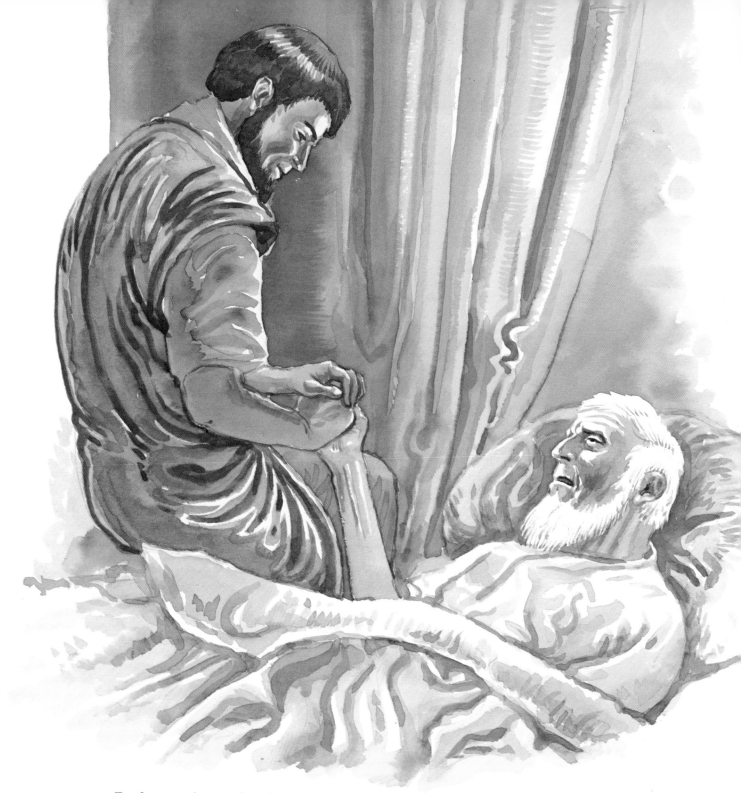

For I was an hungred, and ye gave me meat [food]: I was thirsty, and ye gave me drink: I was a stranger, and ye took me in:

Naked [I had no clothes], and ye clothed me: I was sick, and ye visited me: I was in prison, and ye came unto me.

Then shall the righteous [those who had truly followed Jesus] answer him, saying, Lord, when saw we thee an hungred, and fed *thee*? or thirsty, and gave *thee* drink?

When saw we thee a stranger, and took *thee* in? or naked, and clothed *thee*?

Or when saw we thee sick, or in prison, and came unto thee?

And the King [God] shall answer and say unto them, Verily I say unto you, Inasmuch as ye have done *it* [good deeds] unto one of the least of these my brethren [any person who needed help], ye have done *it* [the same things] unto me.

Matthew 25:35-40

14

The disciples then knew that they could best serve God and Jesus by helping those in need within their own families, neighborhoods, and cities.

Jesus then told his faithful listeners that in two days he would be crucified. It was at this time that Judas, one of the Twelve Apostles, was prompted by Satan to leave the group. He hurried to the temple to find the chief priests. Upon finding them, he told them that if they would give him money, he would help them in their evil plan to destroy Jesus.

THINK ABOUT IT

If we were to meet Jesus, we would treat him with generosity and kindness. How does he expect us to treat other people we meet?

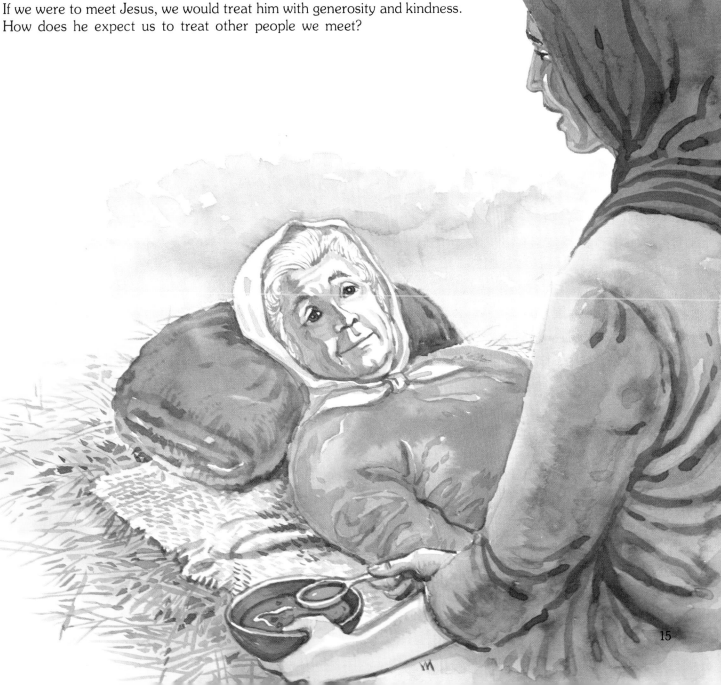

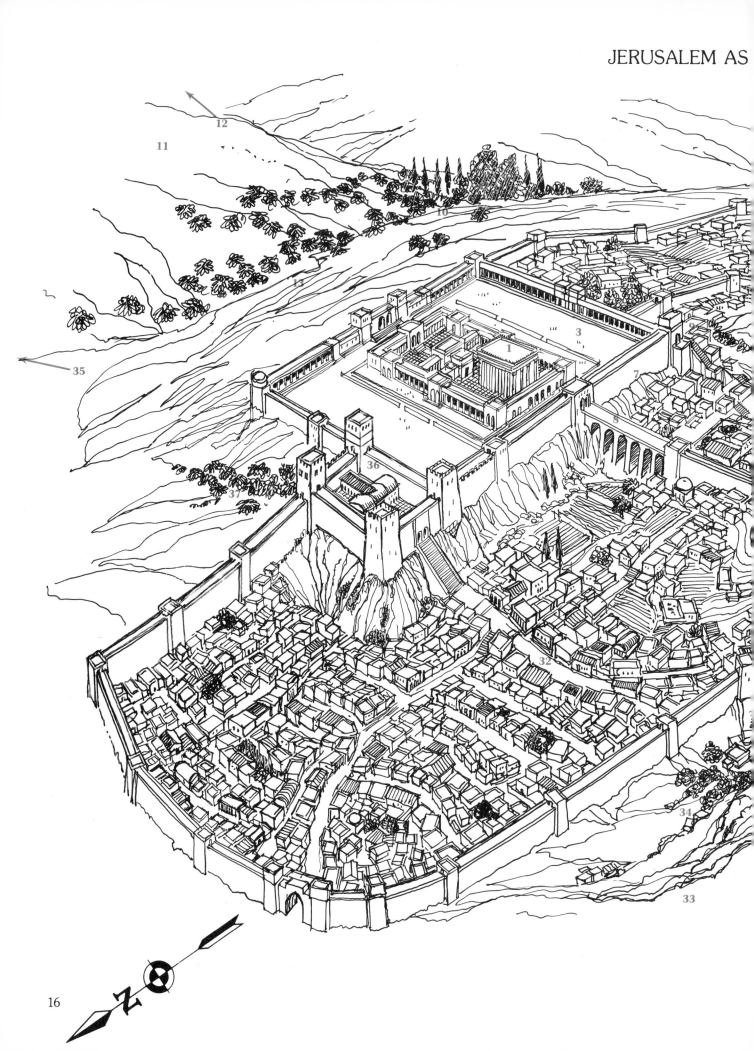

JESUS KNEW IT

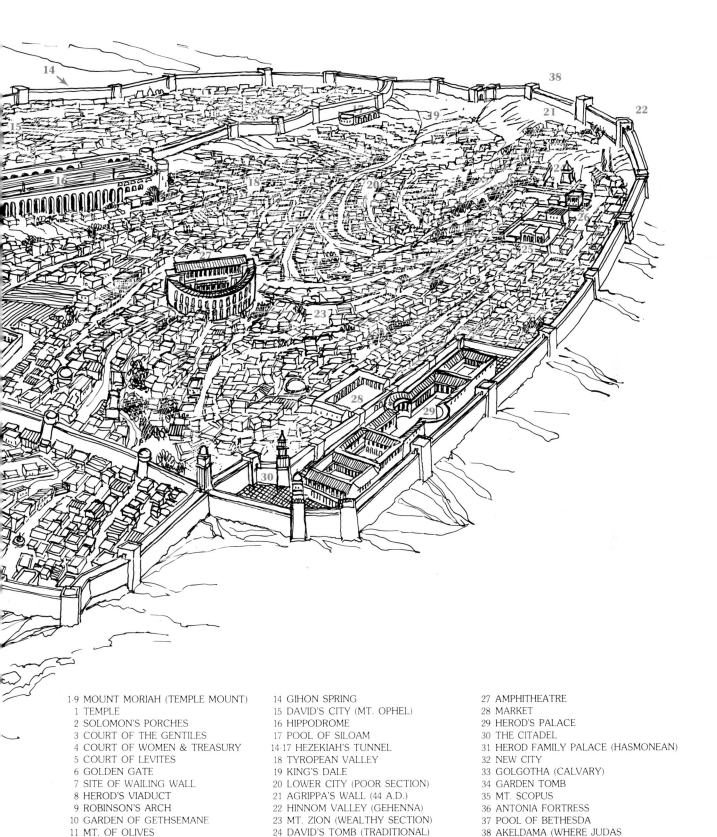

1-9 MOUNT MORIAH (TEMPLE MOUNT)	14 GIHON SPRING	27 AMPHITHEATRE
1 TEMPLE	15 DAVID'S CITY (MT. OPHEL)	28 MARKET
2 SOLOMON'S PORCHES	16 HIPPODROME	29 HEROD'S PALACE
3 COURT OF THE GENTILES	17 POOL OF SILOAM	30 THE CITADEL
4 COURT OF WOMEN & TREASURY	14-17 HEZEKIAH'S TUNNEL	31 HEROD FAMILY PALACE (HASMONEAN)
5 COURT OF LEVITES	18 TYROPEAN VALLEY	32 NEW CITY
6 GOLDEN GATE	19 KING'S DALE	33 GOLGOTHA (CALVARY)
7 SITE OF WAILING WALL	20 LOWER CITY (POOR SECTION)	34 GARDEN TOMB
8 HEROD'S VIADUCT	21 AGRIPPA'S WALL (44 A.D.)	35 MT. SCOPUS
9 ROBINSON'S ARCH	22 HINNOM VALLEY (GEHENNA)	36 ANTONIA FORTRESS
10 GARDEN OF GETHSEMANE	23 MT. ZION (WEALTHY SECTION)	37 POOL OF BETHESDA
11 MT. OF OLIVES	24 DAVID'S TOMB (TRADITIONAL)	38 AKELDAMA (WHERE JUDAS
12 TO BETHPAGE & BETHANY	25 PALACE OF CAIPHAS (TRADITIONAL)	HUNG HIMSELF)
13 KIDRON VALLEY	26 UPPER ROOM (TRADITIONAL)	

THE LAST SUPPER
Washing Feet and Peter's Promise

Jesus and his disciples then left the city of Jerusalem. That night and the next day, which was the fourth day of the week, they stayed in the town of Bethany. On the fifth day of that final week the Jewish people began their great celebration called the Feast of the Passover. This feast is to celebrate the event that happened in the days of Moses when death destroyed the firstborn of all Egyptian families but passed over each Israelite home.

As the sun rose in the east on that quiet morning, a disciple asked Jesus, "Where wilt thou that we go and prepare that thou mayest eat the passover [the food which is the passover feast]?" (Mark 14:12)

Jesus called two of his disciples to him and said, "Go into the city of Jerusalem. As you enter the city, you shall meet a man carrying a pitcher of water. Follow him."

> And wheresoever he shall go in, say ye to the goodman of the house, The Master saith, Where is the guestchamber, where I shall eat the passover with my disciples?
>
> And he will shew you a large upper room furnished *and* prepared: there make ready for us.
>
> And his disciples went forth, and came into the city. . . .

> Mark 14:14-16

Just as Jesus had predicted, they saw a man carrying water, and he led them to the room. The disciples then prepared for the feast.

A few hours later Jesus and the Twelve Apostles gathered to eat the meal that is now called the Last Supper. Before eating, Jesus knelt down and washed the feet of each of these twelve men. He must have felt sorrowful as he washed the feet of Judas, who Jesus knew would soon betray him. When the feet of each disciple had been washed, the group sat down and began to eat.

During the meal Jesus took the cup of wine and prayed, giving thanks to God. Then he gave the cup to one of his disciples, who in turn passed it to another. Jesus then said,

Drink ye all of it;
For this is my blood . . . which is shed for many for the remission of [their] sins.

Matthew 26:27, 28

Peter sensed that Jesus would soon suffer and die. He said to him, "Lord, I am ready to go with thee, both into prison, and to death." (Luke 22:33)

Jesus loved Peter, but he also knew how rough the road ahead would be. As he looked into the eyes of his disciple, he knew that Peter wanted to make such a sacrifice, but that he would not have the strength and courage to do so yet.

Jesus said to him,

I tell thee, Peter, the cock shall not crow this day, before that thou shalt thrice deny that thou knowest me.

Luke 22:34

That night Peter learned, as have so many others, that it is much easier to say what we would like to do than it is to actually do it. Peter wanted to be faithful, and in the months and years that followed he would be. But on this night how could he know the fear he would feel—fear that would cause him to tell those who might harm him that he didn't even know Jesus.

THINK ABOUT IT

1. What did Jesus teach the Twelve Apostles by kneeling before them and washing their feet?
2. Why do you think Peter failed at keeping his word wherein he said to Jesus, "I am ready to go with thee, both into prison, and to death"?

THE LAST SUPPER CONTINUES
Love One Another

As the small group continued eating, Jesus looked at each disciple. When everything was quiet, he softly said, "One of you will betray me." These words must have entered into the heart of Judas like a sword, for he knew Jesus was speaking of him. But the feelings that Satan had placed in his heart were strong, and he was still determined to do his evil work. He looked nervously from side to side. "Then said Jesus unto him, That thou doest, do quickly." (John 13:27)

Judas left the room and ran quickly out into the night.

After Judas was gone, Jesus told the disciples that he would soon leave them. Tears filled their eyes as he said,

A new commandment I give unto you, That ye love one another; as I have loved you, that ye also love one another.

By this shall all *men* know that ye are my disciples, if ye have love one to another.

John 13:34, 35

These good men loved Jesus and he them. After promising his disciples that he would send them the comforting Spirit of the Holy Ghost, the twelve friends sang a hymn. When the last words had been sung, they quietly left the house and walked to the Mount of Olives.

THINK ABOUT IT

How can someone tell if a person is a true disciple of Christ?

JESUS TAKES OUR SINS UPON HIM
The Garden of Gethsemane and the Arrest

Near the Mount of Olives Jesus knelt and looked toward heaven. As he prayed, he told God, his Father, that he had finished the work he had been sent to do. He continued his prayer by asking God to bless his apostles. To this he added,

Neither pray I for [just] these [who are here with me] alone, but for them also [who will come later] which shall believe on me through their word;

That they all [those who believe and follow me] may be one; as thou, Father, *art* in me, and I in thee, that they also may be one in us. . . .

John 17:20, 21

Jesus desired that everyone everywhere, then and now, learn of him and his Father. He prayed that someday all those who followed him would be as "one" in the same kind of love and unity as he and his Father were.

After Jesus had finished praying, he arose from his knees and beckoned for his eleven friends to follow him. The small group then walked to a beautiful garden called Gethsemane. After telling eight of the disciples to wait where they were, he asked Peter, James, and John to follow him to a spot a short distance away.

After they had walked a ways, Jesus stopped, turned toward his three friends, and said,

> My soul is exceeding sorrowful, even unto death; tarry [wait] ye here, and watch with me [while I pray].
>
> And he went a little further, and fell on his face, and prayed, saying, O my Father, if it be possible, let this cup [this painful experience] pass from me [so that I will not have to endure it]: nevertheless [I will do] not as I will, but [I will do] as thou *wilt*.
>
> Matthew 26:38, 39

After this prayer Jesus returned to his disciples and found them asleep.

> He went away again the second time, and prayed, saying, O my Father, if this cup [this painful experience] may not pass away [be taken] from me, except I drink it [suffer it], thy will be done.
>
> Matthew 26:42

After Jesus had made this great promise to God,

> . . . there appeared an angel unto him from heaven, strengthening him.
>
> And being in an agony he prayed more earnestly: and [the pain was so great that] his sweat was as it were great drops of blood falling down to the ground.
>
> Luke 22:43, 44

The agony that filled the soul of Jesus was beyond description. Somehow on that night Jesus Christ, the Son of God, started to take upon himself all the sins of each person who has ever lived.

Through his suffering in Gethsemane, followed by his death on the cross at Calvary, Jesus paid the price for all the sins of those people who would repent and follow him.

Also on this historic occasion the victory Satan had gained in the Garden of Eden was erased. Jesus had made it possible for everyone to experience victory over death and gain eternal life.

When this suffering ended,

And when he rose up from prayer, and was come to his disciples, he found them sleeping for sorrow [and fatigue].

Luke 22:45

Then cometh he to his disciples, and saith unto them, Sleep on now, and take *your* rest: behold, the hour is at hand, and the Son of man is betrayed into the hands of sinners.

Matthew 26:45

THINK ABOUT IT

1. Jesus wanted all his followers to be as "one." What do you think he meant? How can we be as "one"?
2. The greatest desire of Jesus was not to do his own will but to do the will of his Father. What can we learn from that?

THAT WE CAN LIVE AGAIN
The Arrest

In the Garden of Gethsemane Jesus had voluntarily begun to suffer, bleed, and die to pay the price for the sins of all men—that all men might repent, come unto him, and be saved.

He knew that his work was nearly completed. The time to finish the cup he had

begun to drink (his suffering in Gethsemane) was near at hand. Soon would follow his arrest, his trial, his crucifixion, and his death. And with his death the cup (suffering) would be finished.

A brief time later Judas appeared leading the Jewish leaders and a mob of people. Prompted by Satan, Judas ran forward and kissed Jesus on the cheek. This helped the leaders know which of the men was Jesus.

The leaders following closely behind Judas grabbed Jesus and shouted, "You are under arrest."

Peter, not realizing Jesus' work was now nearly completed, could not bear to have his Master arrested. Desperately he drew a sword from a nearby guard and with one quick motion cut off the right ear of the servant of the high priest.

Then said Jesus unto him, Put up again thy sword into his place: for all they that take the sword shall perish with the sword.

Thinkest thou that I cannot now pray to my Father, and he shall presently give me more than twelve legions of angels?

But how then shall the scriptures be fulfilled, that thus it must be?

Matthew 26:52-54

Satan had tried to destroy Jesus earlier but had failed. Now there was no victory in his evil plan, for Jesus walked away with the arresting officers without resistance. Just as he had said, he could have been protected by angels, but that was not his desire. He had agreed to "drink this bitter cup." He knew that in dying he would provide a way for everyone to live again after death.

Perhaps Peter and the others remembered and were beginning to understand what Jesus had said some months earlier:

> Therefore doth my Father love me, because I lay down my life, that I might take it again.
>
> No man taketh it from me, but I lay it down of myself. I have power to lay it down, and I have power to take it again. This commandment have I received of my Father.
>
> John 10:17, 18

THINK ABOUT IT

Why didn't Jesus want Peter and the others to protect him?

37

CLOSE TO THE END
The Trial

When nighttime came to Jerusalem, there were some who did not sleep. Among those walking about during the night whispering quietly to one another were the high priests, the scribes, and the Pharisees. They had long awaited for the opportunity to destroy Jesus and now, sensing that moment near, they could not sleep.

Quickly they assembled to begin a so-called trial—a trial which by law could not be held at night, a trial in which the verdict was decided before the evidence had been considered, a trial of hate and envy.

After questioning Jesus about other matters, the high priest asked,

Art thou the Christ, the Son of the Blessed [God]?

And Jesus said, I am: and ye shall see the Son of man sitting on the right hand of power, and coming in the clouds of heaven.

Then the high priest . . . saith, What need we any further witnesses?

Ye have heard the blasphemy: what think ye? And they all condemned him to be guilty of death [to be put to death].

Mark 14:61-64

THE SORROW OF AN UNKEPT PROMISE
Peter's Denial

Outside of Jerusalem shepherds were watching over their flocks. But this night was different than that night thirty-three years earlier. This night there was no new star in the sky, nor did angels sing.

Within the walls of the Holy City Jesus stood blindfolded. While evil men spit in his face and struck him with the palms of their hands, they asked him with mocking voices, "Tell us who it is that's hitting thee?"

Somewhere else in the city Jesus' friend, Peter—the man who had promised never to deny him—would soon turn away, as Jesus had said he would, leaving Jesus alone to face his painful fate. Even though Peter wanted to be loyal and brave, when he saw what was happening, he became frightened and began to weaken.

A crowd had gathered awaiting the verdict that was to be handed down to Jesus. As they sat around a newly kindled fire, Peter gazed into the flickering flames, wondering, "What can I do? How can I help? What will happen to me if I try to do anything?"

Suddenly a surge of fear swept into Peter's heart, as a woman shouted hatefully and pointed at him, "This man was also with him." (Luke 22:56)

With everyone looking at him, Peter said without thinking, "Woman, I know him not." (Luke 22:57)

After the people had turned their attention away from Peter, he moved back from the fire and kept his head down so that no one else would recognize him.

But to his dismay, a man standing nearby spoke up, "Thou art also of them." Only a few heard this man's accusing words. Peter spoke in a low voice for those around him to hear, "No! I am not one of his followers."

As time dragged by, Peter felt uneasy. Soon it would be daylight and this, the longest night of Peter's life, would be over.

The eastern sky was gradually becoming lighter. Peter looked up, and as he did so, his face became clearly visible. A man suddenly shouted out, "Of a truth this *fellow* also was with him: for he is a Galilæan." (Luke 22:59)

In panic Peter's voice rang out for all to hear,

> Man, I know not what thou sayest. And immediately, while he yet spake, the cock crew.
>
> And the Lord turned, and looked upon Peter. And Peter remembered the word of the Lord, how he had said unto him, Before the cock crow, thou shalt deny me thrice.
>
> Luke 22:60, 61

It was more than Peter could bear, when he looked up and saw his Master looking at him. The look in Jesus' eyes burned into Peter's heart. Peter hurried out, placed his hands on his face, and cried.

The stress of the past few days had been too much for Peter. He had finally done what he had vowed he would never do. He had denied knowing Jesus. Through his tears he promised never again to deny Jesus. And this time, as we shall learn later, he kept his vow.

THINK ABOUT IT

1. Can you ever turn disobedience and the resulting sorrow into something beneficial?
2. How did Jesus "pay" for our sins?
3. How did his dying "save" us from death and the grave?

KING OF THE JEWS
Jesus before Pilate

A great clamor arose when Jesus was led past the crowd. People pushed to get a closer look. Jesus' hands were bound and he appeared helpless, as he was pushed and pulled toward the palace of the Roman leader, Pilate.

Some moments later Jesus was standing before this man, who would later be the one to decide whether Jesus was to live or die.

Pilate listened as the chief priest spoke with all the power that he could muster: "This man claims that he is the King of the Jews. He won't pay taxes to our true king, Caesar."

While the angry Jewish leader's voice became filled with more hatred, Pilate stared at Jesus. Finally he raised his hand to silence the wicked accuser. Pilate then asked Jesus, "Art thou the King of the Jews? And Jesus said unto him, Thou sayest." (Matthew 27:11)

Wishing to avoid condemning a man who seemed so harmless, the Roman leader spoke again, this time to the Jewish leader, "Take ye him, and judge him according to your law." (John 18:31)

At this suggestion the chief priest raised his voice excitedly, saying, "No! We do not want that. It is against our law to put any man to death."

Pilate sensed this evil and jealous man's desire to see Jesus put to death. Again he asked Jesus,

> Art thou the King of the Jews?
>
> Jesus answered, My kingdom is not of this world: if my kingdom were of this world, then would my servants fight, that I should not be delivered to the Jews. . . .
>
> Pilate therefore said unto him, Art thou a king then? Jesus answered, Thou sayest that I am a king. To this end was I born, and for this cause came I into the world, that I should bear witness unto the truth. . . .
>
> John 18:33, 36, 37

THINK ABOUT IT

In what way do you feel Jesus was a king?

SILENT SUFFERING
Jesus Before Herod

Pilate turned to the Jewish leaders and said, "I find in him no fault *at all.*" (John 18:38) To this he added, "He is from Galilee and should be judged by the leaders there. Take him to Herod and see what he wants to do with him."

When Herod (the one who had had John the Baptist killed) saw Jesus, he was glad to finally meet this famous man. When the evil leader asked Jesus questions, Jesus refused to speak a single word.

Herod, angered at Jesus' silence, ordered a beautiful robe to be placed upon Jesus. Then he and his men mocked Jesus by saying, "There now, that is more like it. A king should have a robe. Now you look more like a king."

Jesus remained silent. When Herod and his men had finished mocking him, Herod "sent him again to Pilate." (Luke 23:11)

THE SADDEST SENTENCE
Pilate Gives In

Pilate's wife had told him only moments before:

> Have thou nothing to do with that just man [Jesus]: for I have suffered many things this day in a dream because of him.
>
> Matthew 27:19

Pilate was beside himself, wondering what to do. He didn't want Jesus to die, but he was also afraid that if he went against the Jewish leaders' wishes, the people would revolt. Then Pilate would be in trouble with Caesar.

Perhaps there was one last way out. Pilate knew that it was the custom of the Jews at that time of year to let one prisoner go free.

> And there was *one* [prisoner] named Barabbas, *which lay* bound . . . [in prison because he had committed murder].
>
> Mark 15:7

Pilate said, "You all know the evil man Barabbas. I will let you choose. Would you prefer to release a cruel convict or Jesus, who has done nothing wrong?"

To Pilate's amazement and bitter disappointment the leaders cried out, "Release Barabbas!" Soon all were shouting, "Release Barabbas!"

Pilate shook his head in disbelief. He realized now that the leaders wanted Jesus to die because they feared his great power and popularity. Looking forlornly at the people, Pilate asked,

What will ye then that I shall do *unto him* whom ye call the King of the Jews?
And they cried out again, Crucify him.

Mark 15:12, 13

THINK ABOUT IT

1. What would you have said or done if you had been in the crowd when they cried out, "Crucify him"?
2. What can you do if people around you don't seem to want Jesus as part of their lives?

THAT WHICH CANNOT
BE WASHED AWAY
The Scourging of Jesus

Pilate, convinced of Jesus' innocence, did not want to be responsible for his death. However, he also did not want to offend the wicked Jewish leaders, who were filled with envy and malice.

Once more the Roman leader appealed to the people to release Jesus, but they would not allow it.

> When Pilate saw that he could prevail nothing, but *that* rather a tumult was made [the crowd became even more demanding], he took water, and washed *his* hands before the multitude, saying, I am innocent of the blood of this just person: see *ye to it.*
>
> Matthew 27:24

Pilate washed his hands as a symbol that he would no longer be responsible for what they were about to do. However, Pilate knew, as we do, that some things cannot be washed away with water. Pilate watched sadly as they led Jesus away.

Jesus had already suffered a great deal of anguish. The arrest, the unlawful trial, the mocking by the Jewish high priest, the torment of Herod—all these experiences had caused Jesus great sorrow. Yet this was only a sample of the suffering that was now to come.

The leaders now had what they wanted. The soldiers of Rome were ready to do their unpleasant duty. After scourging (whipping) Jesus, they placed a scarlet robe upon him. One man shouted at Jesus, "You said you were a king. There now, that makes you look more like a king."

Another shouted, "A king needs a crown."

And when they had platted [made] a crown of thorns, they put *it* upon his head, and a reed in his right hand. . . .

Matthew 27:29

One of the guards then knelt in front of Jesus and shouted mockingly, "Hail to you, oh great King of the Jews." Another guard grabbed the reed Jesus was holding in his hand and struck him with it.

So it was that Jesus Christ, the Son of God, was condemned to die. Satan had worked through the hearts of the Jewish leaders to bring the mortal life of Jesus to an end. Although Jesus could have called down angels from heaven for protection, that was not to be. It was in dying that Jesus would accomplish the purpose for which he had been sent from heaven.

THINK ABOUT IT

Could Pilate really wash his hands of what he'd done? Why can't we do wrong and then just walk away as if nothing had happened?

THE SADDEST OF
ALL TIMES
The Crucifixion

Jesus was led from the palace of Pilate. Once outside he was forced to bend over and put his shoulder under the heavy timbers of a cross. With great effort he stood up and took several steps forward. But the weight was too much for him to carry in his weakened condition.

A guard shouted, "Stand up and carry it." But Jesus' body lacked the strength because of the extreme suffering he had undergone. Looking toward a man named Simon who was nearby, the guard shouted, "You there, come over here and carry this cross for him!"

Simon willingly moved forward and picked up the cross. The group moved on again toward a hill called Golgotha. It was at this hill, which had the shape of a skull, that Jesus would be crucified.

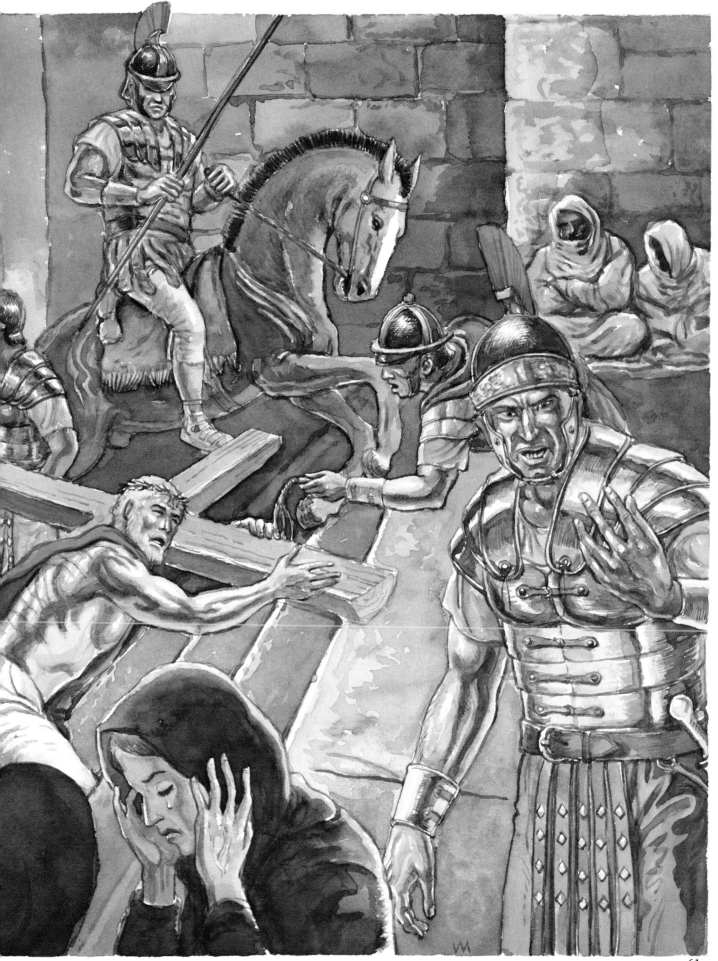

Jesus' followers helplessly listened, as the sounds of the mallet driving the nails through the hands and feet of Jesus broke the silence.

Jesus' cross was pulled up and placed against the sky. Then two more crosses went up, each bearing the body of a thief.

As the crowd moved away, the mother of Jesus and others came closer and wept. They wanted to be near Jesus, yet they did not want to watch him suffer. As they looked up at him, they were amazed to hear Jesus say, "Father, forgive them; for they know not what they do. . . ." (Luke 23:34)

A few minutes later one of the thieves cried out to Jesus in pain, saying,

If thou be Christ, save thyself and us.
But the other [thief] answering rebuked him, saying. . . .
. . . we receive the due reward of our deeds [we deserve to be here]: but this man hath done nothing amiss [wrong].
And he said unto Jesus, Lord, remember me when thou comest into thy kingdom.
And Jesus said unto him, Verily I say unto thee, To day shalt thou be with me in paradise.

Luke 23:39-43

Jesus looked down to where his mother stood by one of his disciples. With great love for this woman, who had done so much for him, he tenderly said to the disciple,

Behold thy mother! And from that hour that disciple took her unto his own *home* [and cared for her as if she were his mother].

John 19:27

As Jesus hung on the cross, the skies gradually became darker until they had the appearance of night, and yet it was the middle of the day! This darkness lasted for three hours.

At the end of this three hours of suffering Jesus cried out with a loud voice, "Father, into thy hands I commend my spirit. . . ." (Luke 23:46) After saying this, Jesus died.

One of the Roman guards, hearing the final words of Jesus, said softly to his friend, "Truly this man was the Son of God." (Mark 15:39)

Nightfall was coming. To make certain that Jesus was dead, a soldier thrust his spear into Jesus.

The crucifixion was over and people returned to their homes. The Jewish leaders were relieved, but the followers of Jesus mourned.

THINK ABOUT IT

Why do you feel the Roman guard said, "Truly this man was the Son of God?"

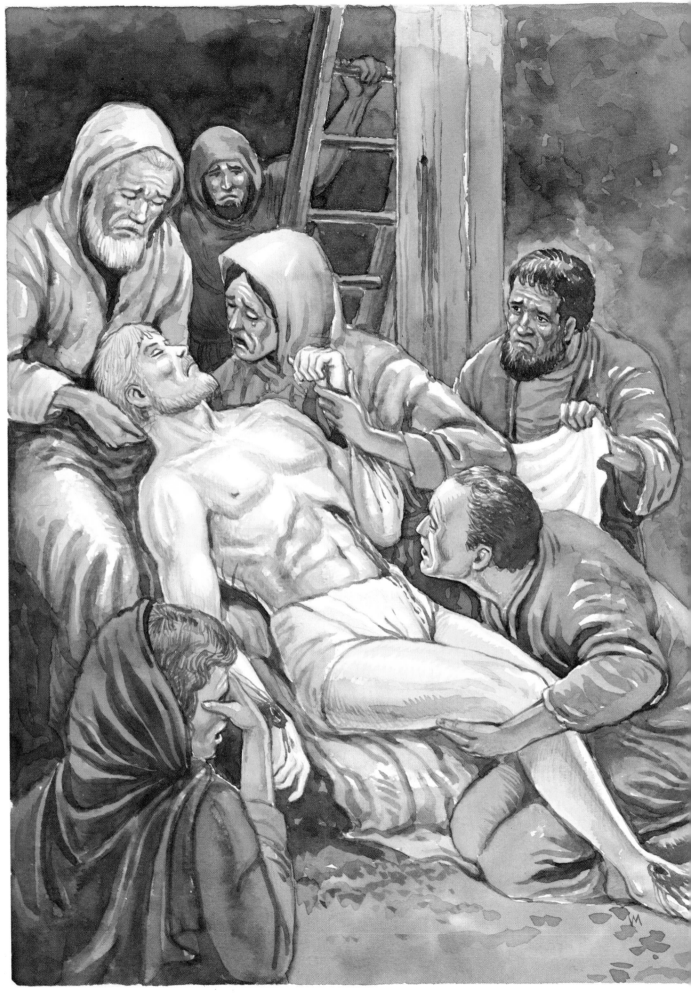

THE HAPPIEST OF ALL TIMES
The Resurrection

A rich man named Joseph of Arimathæa, who had watched Jesus die, hurried to Pilate. He asked Pilate for permission to take Jesus' body to a tomb he owned in which no one had yet been buried.

Mary Magdalene stood by with other women as they watched where the body of Jesus was laid. These women could not prepare the body for burial because it was past sundown and the Jewish Sabbath had begun. They could not do any work that night or the next day because of the Sabbath, but on the following morning they would come to prepare Jesus' body for burial.

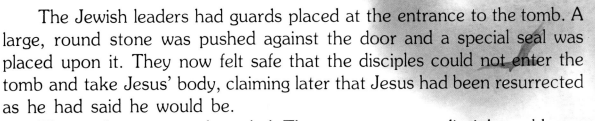

The Jewish leaders had guards placed at the entrance to the tomb. A large, round stone was pushed against the door and a special seal was placed upon it. They now felt safe that the disciples could not enter the tomb and take Jesus' body, claiming later that Jesus had been resurrected as he had said he would be.

The tomb was securely sealed. There was no way a disciple could pass by the guards and roll away the massive stone from the door. But what of angels? Neither guards, stones, nor seals can keep heavenly messengers from going where they desire to go.

And, behold, there was a great earthquake: for the angel of the Lord descended
from heaven, and came and rolled back the stone from the door, and sat upon it.
His countenance was like lightning, and his raiment [clothes] white as snow:
And for fear of him the keepers [guards] did shake, and became as dead *men*.

Matthew 28: 2-4

Jesus had died on Friday. His body had been in the tomb part of that first day and all the second—the Sabbath of the Jews. Early on the third day—the first day of the week—the spirit of Jesus reentered his body and he became alive again.

Jesus Christ, on that first Easter day, was the first person to be resurrected. Because he paid for the sin of the Fall of Adam, every person who ever lives on this earth will also be resurrected. Also, in paying for our own sins, Jesus has made it possible for those who follow him to again live with their Father in heaven.

THINK ABOUT IT

What is an appropriate manner in which to celebrate Easter?

THE FIRST TO KNOW
Mary Sees the Resurrected Christ

Mary Magdalene had scarcely slept for the past two nights. Arising from her bed early Sunday morning, she dressed quickly and hurried off toward the tomb where her beloved Master lay.

As she came closer, she could see by the first glimmer of light that something was wrong. "What has happened," she wondered, as she cautiously approached. "Where is the stone? Why is the tomb open? Who has been here?"

After staring a few moments, Mary turned and began to run. Soon she was at Peter's door shouting for him to awaken.

Peter and John wondered why Mary was so upset. They were astonished and angered when she told them, "They have taken our Lord from the sepulchre (tomb), and we don't know where they have put him."

Peter and John hurried to the tomb. As they approached, they saw that Mary was right—the stone had been rolled away. Stooping down, John looked into the tomb and whispered, "The linen clothes are lying there, but the body is gone."

As the two were returning home, they wondered what could have happened. They had heard Jesus say repeatedly that he would rise again, but they hadn't understood what he had meant. "Someone must have taken the body," they said softly to one another.

Mary returned to the entrance of the tomb. She must have felt that her heart would break. Her Master and Savior had done so much for her. He had made her want to do better and to make her life one of goodness. Now these evil men had not only destroyed him, but someone had taken his body. It was more than she could bear.

She came closer and, hoping to find that his body had been returned, looked into the tomb. What she saw caused her to tremble. For there, sitting on the place where the body of Jesus had been, were two angels. Before she could take a step backwards, one of them spoke:

Woman, why weepest thou? She saith unto them, Because they have taken away my Lord, and I know not where they have laid him.

John 20:13

At that moment Mary heard someone behind her. Turning quickly about, she saw a man she did not recognize. He spoke to her:

Woman, why weepest thou? whom seekest thou? She, supposing him to be the gardener, saith unto him, Sir, if thou have borne him hence [taken the body of Jesus somewhere else], tell me where thou hast laid him, and I will take him away.

John 20:15

Then Jesus spoke one word, "Mary." She stood erect and her heart pounded within her. She knew the voice was that of Jesus!

She cried out, "Master." This woman was the first to know that Christ the Lord had risen from the dead. The gate to eternal happiness at last was open to all.

THINK ABOUT IT

If you could talk to Mary, what three questions would you ask her?

OUR HEARTS CAN BURN WITHIN US
The Disciples on the Road to Emmaus

Sometime later two of Jesus' disciples were walking down a dusty road on their way to the village of Emmaus. "And they talked together of all these things which had happened." (Luke 24:14) Then, without the two of them realizing where he came from, a man joined them and walked and talked with them.

The man was Jesus, but the disciples did not recognize him.

Jesus asked them why they seemed so sad. One of them, whose name was Cleopas, replied by asking,

> Art thou only a stranger in Jerusalem, and hast not known the things which are come to pass there in these days?
> And he said unto them, What things?
>> Luke 24:18, 19

They then told their new companion of the great disappointment they were feeling because Jesus had died without redeeming Israel.

Jesus then said to them, "O fools, and slow of heart to believe all that the prophets have spoken." (Luke 24:25) Then, beginning with Moses, he explained all that the prophets had said about the promised Messiah.

By now they were nearly to the village. The two men invited the stranger (Jesus) to stay with them, saying: "Abide with us: for it is toward evening, and the day is far spent." (Luke 24:29) Jesus agreed to go with them.

Later as they sat eating, "he [Jesus] took bread, and blessed *it*, and brake, and gave to them." (Luke 24:30)

The disciples looked upon him,

And their eyes were opened, and they knew him; and he vanished out of their sight.

Luke 24:31

After Jesus had gone, one of the disciples said to the other, "While we walked with him, my heart burned within me." The other remembered and said, "When he opened the scriptures to me, my heart burned too." These two humble men had had the blessing of being with the resurrected Lord.

THINK ABOUT IT

1. What do you think it means to have your heart "burn" within you?
2. Why did Jesus return and abide with these two disciples? How can we invite him to abide with us?

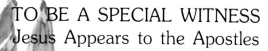

TO BE A SPECIAL WITNESS
Jesus Appears to the Apostles

The two disciples could not sleep. They decided to return to Jerusalem to tell the apostles what had happened.

They found the apostles and were happy to hear that Jesus had also appeared to Peter. They told of their experience along the road and at their home in Emmaus.

> And as they thus spake, Jesus himself stood in the midst of them, and saith unto them, Peace *be* unto you.
>
> Luke 24:36

The appearance of Jesus came so suddenly and unexpectedly that those in the room were terrified at first.

Jesus spoke again and asked,

> Why are ye troubled? and why do thoughts arise in your hearts?
>
> Behold my hands and my feet, that it is I myself: handle me, and see; for a spirit hath not flesh and bones, as ye see me have.
>
> Luke 24:38, 39

Jesus then asked for food,

> And they gave him a piece of a broiled fish, and of an honeycomb.
>
> And he took *it*, and did eat before them.
>
> Luke 24:42, 43

Jesus taught them how the scriptures explained that he would suffer and die and rise from the dead the third day.

He told them that from then on they were to work as special witnesses, telling others that in truth these things had happened. They accepted this challenge, for they did indeed now know that Jesus had risen from the dead.

WE KNOW HIM WITH OUR HEARTS
Thomas Doubts

Thomas was disappointed that he had not been present when Jesus had appeared. As the others told him about it, he said, "I wish I had been there." He added,

Except I shall see in his hands the print of the nails, and put my finger into the print of the nails, and thrust my hand into his side, I will not believe.

John 20:25

Eight days later, while Thomas was with the apostles, Jesus appeared again. He knew what Thomas had said and invited Thomas to feel the nail prints in his hands and the wound in his side. After feeling the scars, Thomas said with deep emotion,

My Lord and my God.
Jesus saith unto him, Thomas, because thou hast seen me, thou hast believed: blessed *are* they that have not seen, and *yet* have believed.

John 20:28, 29

Many were allowed to see the resurrected Christ. It would have been a privilege to have been there on the road to Emmaus or with the apostles in the upper room when he appeared. We were not there, yet our hearts have burned within us as we have felt his presence with us and as we have studied the scriptures. We too are his witnesses that he lived, died, and lives again.

We are deeply blessed, and although we have not seen with our eyes or felt with our hands, yet we know him, and in knowing him we have our joy for eternal life.

THINK ABOUT IT

Why is Thomas sometimes called Doubting Thomas? How are many people far more doubting than was Thomas?

THE POWER TO BEGIN
Jesus Promises the Holy Ghost and Is Taken into Heaven

Forty days had passed since Jesus had come forth from his burial tomb. During this forty days he had appeared often and taught "the apostles whom he had chosen." (Acts 1:2)

Now as the apostles were here again assembled with Jesus, Peter was troubled. He sensed that Jesus would soon depart from them. He knew that he and the others would be left to guide Jesus' followers, and Peter wondered if he would be equal to the task that lay ahead.

Sorrow filled his heart as he remembered how he had denied Christ three times. "Will I fail him again?" he wondered.

Then into his mind came the words that Jesus had spoken on that night of sorrow,

> . . . I have prayed for thee, that thy faith fail not: and when thou art converted, strengthen thy brethren.

> Luke 22:32

Peter's soul filled with hope as he remembered the challenge the resurrected Jesus had given him a few days earlier on the seashore. Jesus had asked him three times, "Peter, lovest thou me?" Each time Peter had replied, "Yea, Lord; thou knowest that I love thee." (John 21:16)

Three times Jesus had answered with words that went deep into Peter's heart, saying, "Feed my sheep [teach the people about me and my Father]." (John 21:17)

Over and over again Peter heard these challenging words in his mind, "Feed my sheep. Feed my sheep."

Peter was now ready to become a teacher. He was ready to feed the flock of God. He was converted, and from this time on he would never again deny Christ.

Suddenly Peter's time for quiet thinking was over. Jesus was speaking. Through the hushed stillness came these words from the Son of God:

> But ye shall receive power, after that the Holy Ghost is come upon you: and ye shall be witnesses unto me . . . unto the uttermost part of the earth.
>
> And when he had spoken these things, while they beheld, he was taken up; and a cloud received him out of their sight.

Acts 1:8, 9

As Peter and the others watched, they heard a voice that caused them to look away from the cloud. Two heavenly messengers dressed in white robes stood nearby. Peter heard one of them say,

. . . this same Jesus, which is taken up from you into heaven, shall so come in like manner [come back someday in the same way] as ye have seen him go into heaven.

Acts 1:11

Peter knew that he and the others had much to do before Jesus returned. But someday, sometime, Peter knew that Christ would fulfill his promise—that he would return to dwell forever upon the earth as its King.

After discussing with the others what they had just seen, Peter said gently, "Come, let us return to Jerusalem." The others followed. Somehow they knew that they were now just beginning the great work Jesus had been preparing them to do.

THINK ABOUT IT

1. Why was Peter so much stronger now than he had been earlier?
2. How can we prepare for the time when Christ will return again?

A LINK WITH HEAVEN
The Holy Ghost

As Peter, James, and John planned for the future, Peter spoke: "Remember his promise to us when he said,"

> And I will pray the Father, and he shall give you another Comforter, that he may abide with you for ever.
>
> John 14:16

Peter continued, "He told us the Comforter, which is the Holy Ghost, would teach us all things and bring all things to our remembrance."

John, who had been listening intently, added, "He also told us that when the Holy Ghost comes upon us, he will testify to us and to others that Jesus is indeed the Son of God."

The apostles felt their souls burn within them, and they knew that what they were now ordained to teach was indeed the truth. All of these humble leaders knew that Jesus had left them with a special inward blessing that would give them power to take the gospel to all the world. There was now a link between these men and the heavens. That link was the promised Comforter—the Holy Ghost.

THE OUTPOURING OF THE HOLY SPIRIT
The Day of Pentecost

The day of Pentecost was the day the Jewish people celebrated their harvest and gave special thought to the law given to Moses on Mount Sinai. Many Jewish people gathered in Jerusalem from near and distant countries. Although not all who had gathered for the traditional feast spoke the same language, they all felt united because they were sharing in this great celebration.

The day began like many other celebrations or feast days, but it was not to end in an ordinary way. God had chosen this day for the outpouring of his Holy Spirit.

As the people gathered in one place,

. . . suddenly there came a sound from heaven as of a rushing mighty wind, and it filled all the house where they were sitting.

And they were all filled with the Holy Ghost, and began to speak with other tongues [languages which they had never spoken before], as the Spirit gave them utterance [through the power of the Holy Ghost].

Acts 2:2, 4

Those who had experienced this great outpouring of heavenly powers went out into the city to tell others. Within a short time thousands had heard the news. As a group of people were discussing their experience, Peter began to speak. While he was speaking, a man whispered to his wife, "That man is speaking in a language that is not spoken in our country and yet I can understand every word he is saying." His wife replied, "I can understand him too, and those people there from a country far to the east also seem to be able to understand him."

And they were all amazed and marvelled, saying one to another, Behold, are not all these which speak Galilæans?

And how hear we every man in our own tongue, wherein we were born?

Acts 2:7, 8

Peter raised his voice, saying, "God promised you that he would pour out his Spirit when he said,"

. . . and your sons and your daughters shall prophesy, and your young men shall see visions, and your old men shall dream dreams:

And I will shew wonders in heaven above, and signs in the earth beneath. . . .

Acts 2:17, 19

Peter continued,

> This Jesus hath God raised up [from the dead], whereof we all are witnesses.
>
> Therefore let all the house of Israel know assuredly, that God hath made that same Jesus, whom ye have crucified, both Lord and Christ.
>
> Acts 2:32, 36

All who were listening to Peter knew by the power of the Holy Ghost that what Peter had said was true. They asked with great desire,

> . . . what shall we do?
>
> Then Peter said unto them, Repent, and be baptized every one of you in the name of Jesus Christ for the remission of sins, and ye shall receive the gift of the Holy Ghost.
>
> Acts 2:37, 38

Peter then spoke to all people in all ages of time by saying,

> For the promise is unto you, and to your children, and to all that are afar off, *even* as many as the Lord our God shall call.
>
> Acts 2:39

After Peter had finished speaking, some three thousand people were baptized. The promise Jesus had made that the Holy Ghost would testify of God the Father and the mission of his Only Begotten Son had been fulfilled.

Peter now understood what Jesus had meant when he had said, "Feed my sheep." He also realized that although many people had been fed the news of the everlasting gospel that day, there were yet many more waiting to hear the important message.

THINK ABOUT IT

1. How can we best become converted?
2. How can we "feed the Lord's sheep" today?

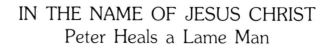

IN THE NAME OF JESUS CHRIST
Peter Heals a Lame Man

In the weeks following Pentecost, Peter and the others felt even more strongly that they were to take the gospel to Jewish people everywhere.

As Peter and John were talking on their way to the temple, their conversation was interrupted by a voice calling out, "Alms for the poor."

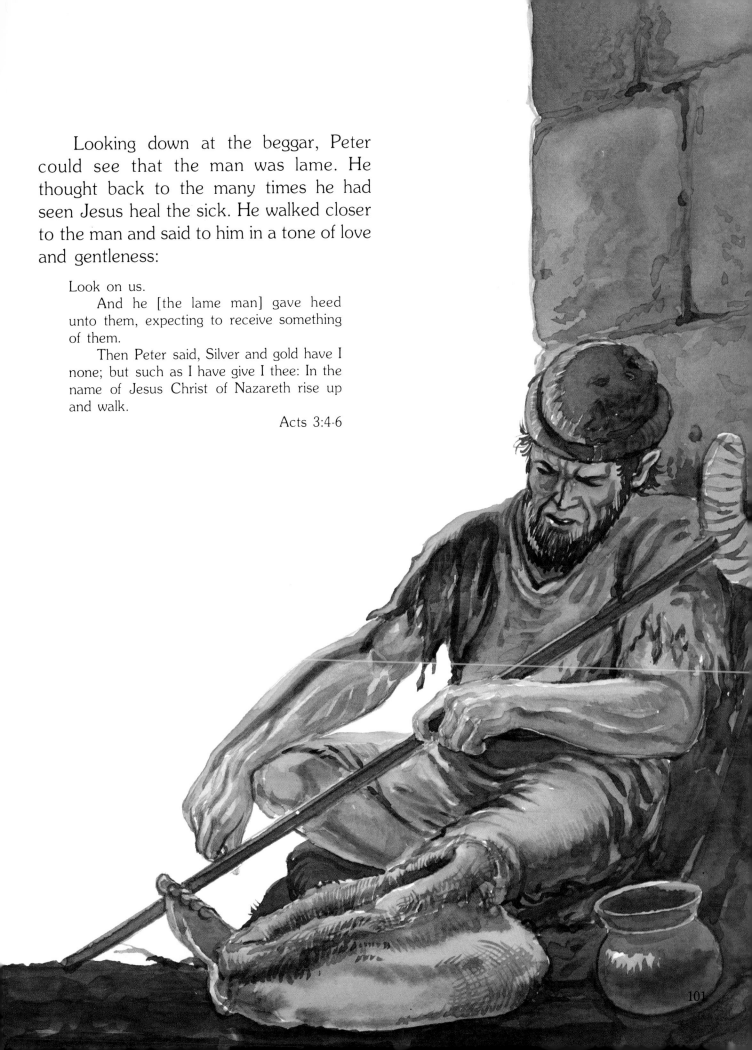

Looking down at the beggar, Peter could see that the man was lame. He thought back to the many times he had seen Jesus heal the sick. He walked closer to the man and said to him in a tone of love and gentleness:

Look on us.

And he [the lame man] gave heed unto them, expecting to receive something of them.

Then Peter said, Silver and gold have I none; but such as I have give I thee: In the name of Jesus Christ of Nazareth rise up and walk.

Acts 3:4-6

And he [Peter] took him by the right hand, and lifted *him* up: and immediately his feet and ankle bones received strength.

And he leaping up stood, and walked, and entered with them into the temple, walking, and leaping, and praising God.

And all the people saw him walking and praising God:

And they knew that it was he which sat for alms at the Beautiful gate of the temple: and they were filled with wonder and amazement at that which had happened unto him.

Acts 3:7-10

Inside the temple people listened carefully to Peter and John. They had seen the miracle and they wondered about the great power these men possessed.

Peter told his listeners that the power he and John possessed came from Jesus Christ. He reminded them that although the Jewish leaders had crucified Christ, Christ had risen from the dead.

He told them, "Repent ye therefore, and be converted, that your sins may be blotted out. . . ." (Acts 3:19) Peter also told them that Jesus would someday come again.

Many believed the words of Peter, but others did not. Those others, whose hearts were guided by Satan, now realized that they had a new threat to their power. Now they must see that the voices of Peter, John, and the other apostles were silenced. From that time on they began to plan how they would bring this about.

THINK ABOUT IT

1. What can we give others if we have no "silver and gold?"
2. Why is such a gift better than money?

GIVING ONE'S LIFE
Stephen Dies for the Cause of Truth

Peter preached with great power everywhere he went. Many joined the Church of Christ, and they all shared what they had with one another. These were happy yet difficult times for Peter and the other members.

However, clouds were gathering and the future would not be without its trials. The Jewish leaders were doing all they could to cause Jesus' followers to give up their belief in him. All those who were baptized as followers of Christ rejoiced "that they were counted worthy to suffer shame [such persecution] for his name." (Acts 5:41) Although they knew it would cause them to be persecuted, "they ceased not to teach and preach Jesus Christ." (Acts 5:42)

The apostles were so busy leading and teaching the newly converted flock that there was little time to tell others who had not yet heard about Jesus. To assist them the apostles chose seven special servants. Among these seven was a man named Stephen.

Stephen was happy with his new call to serve the followers of Christ and to be a missionary. He did his work well, and his faith was unshakable.

Upon finding a crowd of people, Stephen began to preach. At the beginning only a few payed attention, but soon all were listening to what he was saying. Stephen spoke with great power and the people felt that he was speaking the truth.

The Jewish leaders had not been concerned when Stephen had started speaking. But now as they saw that many were listening, they felt they must do something to stop him.

As the leaders came closer, Stephen saw them but continued preaching with great fervor about Jesus and his crucifixion and resurrection.

The Jewish leaders were enraged and shouted at Stephen. Soon others began to feel the same hatred. Someone shouted, "This man should be stoned to death."

At that moment, filled with the Holy Ghost, Stephen looked up into heaven and saw the glory of God. He shouted, "Behold, I see the heavens opened, and the Son of man standing on the right hand of God." (Acts 7:56)

The Jewish leaders would not listen and together they came toward him. Angry men dragged him outside the city and hurled him to the ground.

Some of the men laid down their heavy robes at the feet of a man named Saul. Then, picking up heavy stones, they began throwing them at Stephen. As the stones hit Stephen, he called upon God, saying, "Lord Jesus, receive my spirit." (Acts 7:59) He then knelt down and said with a loud voice, "Lord, lay not this sin to their charge." (Acts 7:60) Then he died.

When Peter heard of Stephen's death, he wept. He knew Stephen had died for the cause of truth, and that there would be others like Stephen in the future. But he also knew that the gospel of Jesus Christ was a cause worth giving up one's life for. He realized that it was a message that would change the world—a message that would make it possible for men to find peace in this life and eternal life with God. Surely these were two important blessings Stephen gained through the sacrifice he made.

THINK ABOUT IT

Why do you feel Stephen was willing to die?

THE GOSPEL OF JESUS IS FOR ALL PEOPLE
The Story of Cornelius

Many Jews had now been taught the truth. But Jesus had said before leaving, "Go ye therefore, and teach all nations, baptizing them in the name of the Father, and of the Son, and of the Holy Ghost." (Matthew 28:19)

Peter felt that the time of the Gentiles—people who were not Jews—had not yet come, and that only the Jews were to be taught of Jesus. In the following manner God helped Peter understand that the gospel of Jesus Christ was for all the people.

A man named Cornelius was living in Jerusalem, although he was not Jewish. He was there as a foreign soldier. He and his family were very good people, giving money to the poor and praying often. However, this man and his family knew little about Christ and were not among his followers.

One day Cornelius was surprised when an angel appeared to him and said, ". . . send men to Joppa, and call for *one* Simon, whose surname is Peter." (Acts 10:5)

Cornelius called two of his servants to him and sent them to Joppa to find Peter. Meanwhile, Peter was having a strange but meaningful dream.

In his dream he saw the heavens open and a great cloth come down in front of him. On the cloth were many four-footed beasts and things that the Jewish people felt were unclean and would not eat.

Peter was surprised when he was told to kill these things and eat them. He refused, saying,

> Not so, Lord; for I have never eaten any thing that is common or unclean.
>   And the voice *spake* unto him again the second time, What God hath cleansed, *that* call not thou common.

Acts 10:14, 15

The dream taught Peter the great lesson that the gospel of Jesus Christ was not just for the Jewish people. It was also for the Gentiles.

Peter was not surprised when the two servants of Cornelius arrived. Hearing that a Gentile had sent for him, he eagerly made his way to Cornelius.

When Peter met this righteous soldier, he said,

Of a truth I perceive that God is no respecter of persons:
    But in every nation he that feareth him [loves God],
and worketh righteousness [does good things], is accepted
with him.

Acts 10:34, 35

He then told Cornelius the story of Jesus.

    While Peter yet spake these words, the Holy Ghost fell on
all them which heard the word.
    And he commanded them to be baptized in the name of
the Lord. . . .

Acts 10:44, 48

The gospel of Jesus Christ is indeed for all men.
Through Peter and others Jesus Christ opened the door
for men and women everywhere and in all times to hear,
accept, and live according to God's teachings.

THINK ABOUT IT

If you were going to tell people about Cornelius, what would you
tell them?

A MIGHTY LEADER
Peter

Influenced by Satan, the Jewish leaders continued to do what they could to crush the rapidly growing group of believers. Another Herod had risen to power. This man was not the Herod who had killed the children some thirty-three years earlier while Jesus was a child, nor was he the one who had murdered John the Baptist. But this Herod was just as wicked as his relatives of the same name had been.

This Herod commanded his men to arrest James, the brother of John. He then had James killed with the sword.

Having pleased the Jewish leaders with this wicked act and wishing to ensure his power further, Herod quickly sent soldiers to arrest Peter.

As the members watched their beloved leader being led away, they wondered how they would carry on without him. They prayed continually for Peter's safe return.

117

The Jewish leaders made sure Peter could not escape from prison. At night he was bound by chains and forced to sleep between two guards, while more were posted at the prison door. There was almost no way for Peter to escape.

But all this prison security was for nothing. Suddenly a bright light lit every corner of the dismal dungeon, and in that light stood an angel. Going over to Peter, the angel said, "Arise up quickly." (Acts 12:7) As Peter arose, the chains fell off his hands.

The angel told Peter to dress quickly and follow him.

Peter wondered if he were dreaming as he cautiously followed the angel. Finally they came to a huge iron gate. As they approach the gate, it

opened to them of his [its] own accord: and they went out, and passed on through one street; and forthwith the angel departed from him.

Acts 12:10

For a few moments Peter thought about what had just happened to him. Then joy filled his heart as he realized that he was free.

Hardly able to contain his excitement, Peter hurried to the house of a woman named Mary, who was the mother of Mark. As Peter knocked on the door, those inside paused in their prayers. Fearing it might be soldiers, a young girl named Rhoda was chosen to go to the door. Thus if it were soldiers, they would go away thinking only one family was there.

Rhoda called out through the closed door, "Who is there?"

Peter replied, "It is me. Open up."

Surprised and excited at hearing Peter's voice, she ran back down the hall and called out, "It's him! It's Peter!"

"You are mistaken child," Rhoda's mother replied. "It can't be Peter. He is in prison."

The knocking was heard again. It was much louder and longer than before.

This time they all went to the door. Tears of joy filled their eyes as they saw Peter before them. Without entering he told them all what had happened. Then, because he had a lot to do, he bid them good night and hurried away.

Peter went on working as an apostle of Jesus Christ, although the Bible says little more about him. Until his death he continued to strengthen the members of the Church. Truly Peter was a rock—a rock of strength and virtue.

FROM PERSECUTING TO PREACHING
Saul's Conversion

Those who believed and were baptized in the name of Jesus Christ were not allowed to go their own way. Stephen, James, Peter, and others were put to death because they would not deny Christ. Those with power in the government spent much of their energy trying to end this new doctrine, which it seemed might destroy the age-old Jewish way of life. Among those determined to stop this growing group of Christians was a man named Saul. This was the same man who had stood by and watched Stephen being stoned.

Because of Saul and others like him, the members of the Church were scattered. Some had left Jerusalem and had gone to other cities. Saul received permission to go to Damascus and bring these people back to stand trial.

As Saul and his men neared Damascus, they were suddenly startled to see a light from heaven shine down directly on Saul.

And he fell to the earth, and heard a voice saying unto him, Saul, Saul, why persecutest thou me?

Acts 9:4

In deep shock Saul asked,

Who art thou, Lord? And the Lord said, I am Jesus whom thou persecutest: *it is* hard for thee to kick against the pricks.

Acts 9:5

Jesus knew that Saul was struggling with his conscience for all the problems he had caused Jesus and his followers. Trembling with fear, Saul asked,

Lord, what wilt thou have me to do? And the Lord *said* unto him, Arise, and go into the city, and it shall be told thee what thou must do.

Acts 9:6

As Saul stood up, his men rushed to him and asked, "What happened? What was it?" Saul replied, "I can't see. My sight is gone." Following the instructions given him by Jesus, he told them to lead him to Damascus.

In that city a man named Ananias had been told in a vision that Saul would soon arrive at a certain house. He, Ananias, was to go to that house to teach him.

And Ananias went his way, and entered into the house; and putting his hands on him said, Brother Saul, the Lord, *even* Jesus, that appeared unto thee in the way as thou camest, hath sent me, that thou mightest receive thy sight, and be filled with the Holy Ghost.

And immediately there fell from his eyes as it had been scales: and he received sight forthwith, and arose, and was baptized.

Acts 9:17, 18

Saul now became known as Paul, and he who had once been so intent upon destroying the Church would soon be responsible for thousands of people becoming faithful followers of Jesus Christ.

Paul went to Jerusalem to meet the apostles. After talking with him, the apostles were both amazed and deeply pleased that their former enemy was now one of them.

Under the direction of the apostles, Paul departed on his first of many missions—missions that would enable him to take the gospel to many new parts of the world.

Paul's life was one of excitement, adventure, and persecution. His hardships included being beaten, stoned, shipwrecked, and robbed. Many times he suffered from hunger, thirst, and cold. Although his life as a missionary was difficult, the people he taught loved him dearly because he brought them the message of Jesus Christ.

Paul traveled from city to city, preaching that Jesus was the Son of God. He also wrote many letters encouraging the converts to remain true to the faith. In these letters Paul explained many doctrines and teachings which had been taught to him by the Holy Ghost. These letters are printed in the Bible and are called The Epistle (letter) of Paul the Apostle to the Romans, the Corinthians, the Galatians, the Ephesians, the Philippians, the Colossians, the Thessalonians, and to Timothy, Titus, and Philemon.

Paul was finally arrested and sent to Rome. While in prison awaiting his trial, he converted many people to the gospel. Finally he was put to death because he would not deny his testimony of Jesus.

THINK ABOUT IT

What is the important message taught to us by the experience of Saul on his way to Damascus?

THE FUTURE
The Book of Revelation

The time came when John was the only apostle still alive. He was sent to an island called Patmos, and while there he saw a vision of the total plan of God. In this revelation he saw into the future to the time when Satan would be bound and no longer able to tempt men. He saw the time when Jesus Christ would return to the earth as King. He saw God's final triumph over Satan, as well as the glorious place prepared for all who love and obey God and his Son, Jesus Christ.

Jesus told John,

> Behold, I stand at the door, and knock: if any man hear my voice, and open the door, I will come in to him, and will sup with him, and he with me.
>
> Revelation 3:20

Jesus stands at our door and knocks. If we invite him into our lives and keep his commandments, we will have peace in this life and eternal life with him in heaven.

LOOKING AHEAD

We have now come to the end of the story as told in the Holy Bible. As our lives unfold, we will want to study the truths of this inspiring book time and again.

As we learn to better understand and live according to the messages of God and his Son, Jesus Christ, we will enjoy feelings of hope and love. We will realize there is no lasting death. We will know that God lives, that he loves us, and that he answers our prayers. We will indeed find the peace that "passeth all understanding."

May God be with you, this day and forever.